T is for Titanic

A Titanic Alphabet

Written by Debbie & Michael Shoulders
Illustrated by Gijsbert van Frankenhuyzen

A is for Anatomy of the Titanic

The RMS *Titanic*
included ten decks in all.
It was the world's largest moving
object at 175 feet tall!

A ship's anatomy tells us about the structure, its parts, and their functions. When the *Titanic* set sail on her maiden voyage in 1912, she was the largest man-made moving object in the world. *Titanic* was designed and constructed to a length of 882 feet and 9 inches long and had ten decks. Decks are the levels, or floors, of a ship. The highest level, boat deck, was the uppermost deck of the ship equipped with officers' quarters, a gymnasium, and outdoor walking areas called promenades. It also stored full-sized lifeboats and two smaller lifeboats. The lowest deck, called the tank top, held the lowermost portions of the cargo holds, boiler rooms, engine rooms, and coal storage. The decks between the tank top and the boat deck on the *Titanic* were given letter names A to G. One of the more unusual names for the ship's anatomy was the poop deck. It was the highest part of the outdoor deck on the ship's stern, or rear. Despite its strange name, there were no toilets there. Its name came from the Latin word, *puppis*, for a cluster of stars shaped like the stern of a ship.

Original plans called for three funnels, or smokestacks. Since more funnels signified extra strength, a fourth funnel was added to make the ship look more powerful. But it had no function except to ventilate the kitchens of the *Titanic*.

The *Titanic* had three anchors, one on each side of the bow, or front of the ship, and a center anchor stored on the forecastle, or fore deck.

B is for Bridge

The *Titanic* had a bridge—
　　the steering was done here.
It sat upon the boat deck
　　where the captain's view was clear.

The bridge is a ship's command center. Open on the sides, it is called the bridge because captains used it as a walkway to observe activities on both sides of the ship. In the mid-1880s glass windows were added to protect the crew from winds and rain. Located on the boat deck, *Titanic*'s bridge came with the newest technology in navigational tools. It held a wheel for steering and brass telegraphs that were used to communicate with other areas of the ship. *Titanic* also had four compasses: one on the bridge, one between funnels two and three, another in the docking bridge, and the final one in the wheelhouse. In the late evening hours of April 14, 1912, lookout Frederick Fleet sighted an iceberg in the path of the *Titanic*. Working from the boat deck, telegraph operator Jack Phillips sent the first distress signal at 12:15 a.m. The first distress call used was CQD. The CQ means "all stations" and the D represents distress. It is also unofficially referred to as "Come Quick Distress."

While first- and second-class passengers might have boarded the *Titanic* as part of a vacation, third-class passengers were often immigrants bound for new opportunities in America. Millvina Dean's family was immigrating to Wichita, Kansas. She was the youngest of *Titanic*'s passengers at only nine weeks old. Millvina survived with her mother and older brother. Later, when sailing back with her mother to England on the *Adriatic*, Millvina was known as "the miracle baby." The first- and second-class passengers were so fascinated with her that they were given orders that she could only be held for ten minutes at a time. With the discovery of the *Titanic*'s remains, Millvina Dean once again became a celebrity and often spoke at public and media events. Before she died at the age of 97, Millvina had become the last survivor of the legendary ship.

Survivor Douglas Spedden was a six-year-old, first-class passenger. He carried a Stieff brand white teddy bear that eventually found its way into his mother's book, *Polar, the Titanic Bear*. Douglas was also photographed, spinning a top, in one of the few remaining photographs taken of passengers aboard the ship.

C is for Children

Children crossed the Atlantic
with dreams all their own—
a new life in America,
new friends, and a new home.

D d

People were not the only passengers on the *Titanic*. Ten dogs were listed on the passenger list with their owners. The *Titanic* provided kennels or allowed smaller animals to stay in the cabins with their owners. Their pets were so treasured that the passengers planned an impromptu dog show to take place during the trip. John Jacob Astor, the richest man on the ship, brought his Airedale terrier, Kitty. American banker Robert W. Daniels had brought along Gamin De Pycombe, a French bulldog. Seven-year-old Eva Hart became fascinated with Gamin, curious about the "flat- faced, bat-eared dog." It took Eva Hart more than 40 years to find the type of dog that she first met on the *Titanic*, but in 1956, she finally found and adopted a French bull-dog that she named Mrs. Huffle Puffle.

As the ship began to sink, the dogs in the kennels were released, but only three dogs survived. Margaret Hays tucked her Pomeranian inside her coat as she left by lifeboat. Publisher Henry Harper saved his Pekingese, Sun Yat Sen. Elizabeth Barrett Rothschild, wife of wealthy businessman Martin Rothschild, boarded a lifeboat with her Pomeranian.

D is for Dogs

Sailing on the *Titanic*
with the captain and his crew
were 1,300 passengers
along with ten dogs, too.

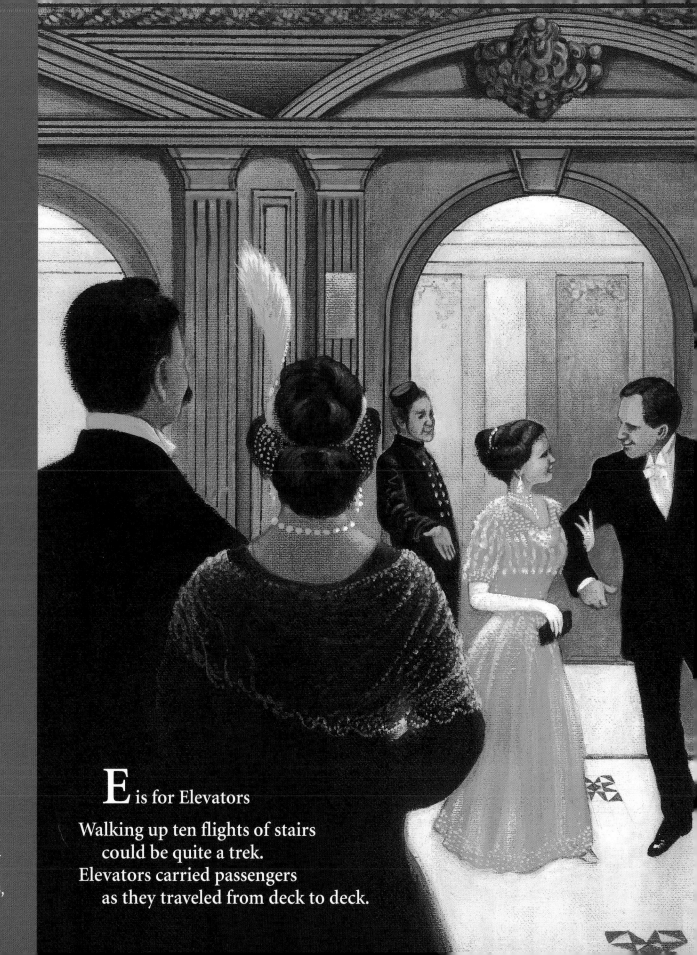

The *Titanic* had a vast number of items that required electricity. From the "Electronic Engine Room" electrical power was sent to operate everything from potato peelers to ice cream makers to cargo cranes. More important to the passengers may have been the four elevators that serviced first- and second-class passengers. Originally the plans called for two lifts, or elevators, to be installed on the *Titanic*, but ultimately four were included. Three elevators, side-by-side, for first-class passengers, were located just forward of the grand staircase. These three elevators traveled 37 feet, 6 inches from A-deck to E-deck. Second-class passengers used a single elevator that ran from the boat deck to E-deck.

While the second-class elevator was popular with its passengers, first-class travelers felt that the elevator quarters were tight and didn't like that the elevator would sometimes stick when the seas were rough. Each elevator had a male attendant: Frederick Allen, age 17, William Carney, age 31, Alfred King, age 18, and Reginald Pacey, age 17. None survived.

E is for Elevators

Walking up ten flights of stairs
could be quite a trek.
Elevators carried passengers
as they traveled from deck to deck.

F f

F is for First Class

First-class passengers on board
had a lot of things to do:
A heated pool, a gymnasium,
and even a library, too.

More than 300 of *Titanic's* first-class passengers enjoyed some luxuries uncommon to passenger ships in the early 1900s. The price of first-class tickets included access to a heated swimming pool, a gymnasium, and a library. Among the first-class passengers were John Jacob Astor, Isidor Straus, and his wife Ida. Straus was a co-owner of Macy's Department Store. Margaret Tobin Brown, the wife of a millionaire, was a women's rights activist who used the wealth from gold discoveries in Colorado to make life better for Denver's citizens. She had to be persuaded to get into a lifeboat as she aided others and continued to comfort those who could not speak English. After her death in 1932 she became known as "the Unsinkable Molly Brown" which later became the title of a Broadway musical.

G is for Grand Staircase

Titanic's elegance and beauty
shined in its grand staircase.
A dome of glass and cherub with flame
created a beautiful space.

Due to the popularity of movies about the *Titanic*, one of the better-known structures from the ship was its grand staircase. There were two staircases in first class, one forward and one aft. There was also a second-class staircase located even further aft of the first-class aft staircase. The forward first-class staircase was the most elaborate. The grand staircase, constructed from solid oak supported by wrought iron grillwork with ornate gilt bronze garlands, was built to represent *Titanic's* opulence. The staircase began at the first-class entrance on the boat deck, continued on to the reception room outside the dining room of D-deck, and concluded at E-deck. Spectators would see on the landing a large carved panel with a clock surrounded by two classical figures, one representing Honor and the other Glory, each depicted crowning Time. Above the staircase was a wrought iron and glass dome fashioned so that natural light could filter in. At night, electric lights simulated sunlight to perpetually fill the space with light. The flooring of the staircase was made of the most innovative, high-quality floor covering of that time—linoleum.

H h

Harland & Wolff Ltd, led by the Right Honorable Lord Pirrie, was one of the largest shipbuilding companies in Europe. Located in Belfast, Ireland, Harland & Wolff's ship-yard employed 15,000 workers, thousands of whom worked five-and-a-half days a week on the giant ship starting in March of 1909. The company built the *Titanic*, as well as her two sister ships, HMHS *Britannic* and RMS *Olympic*. The realization of this gigantic adventure began at a dinner party late in the summer of 1907. Lord Pirrie and J. Bruce Ismay, director of the White Star Line, wanted to compete with the size and luxury of Cunard's ocean liners. The idea was to think big, literally, and to build the largest passenger ship ever! In addition to being large, this ship would also offer elegant, safe accommodations.

H is for Harland & Wolff

Shipbuilders Harland & Wolff
constructed colossal ships
to provide luxurious sailing
on transatlantic trips.

While it was not unusual to see ice floating in the North Atlantic during the spring months, seeing an iceberg meant real danger. Icebergs are chunks of ice that calve (break off) from glaciers, ice shelves, or larger icebergs, and they can be very dangerous to ships.

The *Titanic*'s wireless radio picked up iceberg warnings from another passenger ship, the *Caronia,* and a Dutch liner, *Noordam,* on the morning of April 14, 1912. At 11:40 that night, when the ship was within 400 miles of Newfoundland, Canada, lookout Frederick Fleet sighted an iceberg in *Titanic*'s path. Fleet rang a warning bell and telephoned the bridge, saying, "Iceberg right ahead!"

First Officer William Murdoch telegraphed the engine room telling them, "Stop!" while ordering Quartermaster Robert Hichens to steer the ship to port, or left. Unfortunately, the huge iceberg grazed the ship on the front starboard, or right side. Passenger aware-ness of the collision varied. Some passengers in third class felt a sharp jolt, but others in first class felt nothing. Fleet and Hichens made it safely to lifeboats, but Murdoch succumbed to the cold of the Atlantic.

I i

I is for Iceberg

Late in the evening
as the *Titanic* sailed due west,
the lookout shouted "Iceberg right ahead!"
from atop the tall crow's nest.

J j

J is for J. Bruce Ismay

The White Star Line built *Titanic*
    Its leader was named Ismay.
He was on the maiden voyage
    as the dream ship sailed away.

Joseph Bruce Ismay was the director of the White Star Line, the company that owned the *Titanic* and its two sister ships. He collaborated with Lord Pirrie to construct three passenger vessels that would be larger and more sumptuous than rival Cunard's *Lusitania* and *Mauretania*. On April 10, 1912, J. Bruce Ismay became one of the first passengers to board the *Titanic* and move into his luxurious parlor suite with a private promenade deck. When Captain Smith received telegrams warning of ice in the area on April 14, he showed one to Ismay. A total of five ice warnings were received the same day, while other reports had been received by the bridge beginning on the 12th.

Later Ismay was on hand helping people into lifeboats. He left on one of the last lifeboats, Collapsible C. In the aftermath of the tragedy, many blamed J. Bruce Ismay, saying that he had insisted that Captain Smith maintain a higher than safe speed for the conditions, and that he should have remained aboard the *Titanic*. Ultimately no fault was found with his behavior. Ismay spent the rest of his life out of the public eye and allowed no mention of the *Titanic* in his presence.

K is for Kodak Camera

Recording historic moments
on this ship's first journey
was a Kodak camera.
It made pictures for all to see.

Father Francis Browne, a 32-year-old Jesuit priest, received an extraordinary gift from his uncle, the Bishop of Cloyne: a first-class ticket for the first leg of *Titanic*'s maiden voyage. Father Browne was also an amateur photographer with a Kodak camera. Beginning with pictures at Waterloo Station, where many passengers began their trip, Browne continued to take photographs on board the ship, where he recorded daily activities of passengers and crew, and ended with pictures of the anchor being raised for the final time. The fact that the pictures are available today is something of a miracle. Father Browne was invited to remain on the ship to America but was ordered by his superiors to disembark at Queenstown, Ireland, as planned. He stored the *Titanic* negatives in a metal trunk, where they remained until after his death in 1960. Father E. E. O'Donnell discovered the pictures in 1986! Although half of the negatives were unstable and had deteriorated, duplicates were made. Father Browne's pictures remain a visual narrative of life aboard the *Titanic*.

K
k

L1

L is for Lifeboats and Lifebelts

Passengers may use these
as a safe way to float.
If there's trouble while at sea
find lifebelts and lifeboats.

Lifeboats and lifebelts—known today as life jackets—became extremely important when passengers and crew realized they were their only hope of survival. At 28° F, the ocean water temperature was too cold for anyone to survive for more than a few minutes.

Early plans for the construction of the *Titanic* included 64 lifeboats. The owners reduced that number to 32 and then to 16 to allow more room for deck space. There were also four Englehardt collapsible boats for a total of 20 lifeboats. There was not enough room in the lifeboats to handle the more than 2,200 passengers and crew on board the *Titanic*. However, there were enough lifebelts. John Jacob Astor helped his wife into her lifebelt and onto a lifeboat. Madeleine Astor, pregnant with her first child, kept the lifebelt on until Dr. Gottlieb Rencher took her into his care aboard the rescue ship, the *Carpathia*. Only then, did Madeleine take off her protective covering. The Rencher family later donated the lifebelt to the Titanic Historical Society.

The invention of the wireless radio by Guglielmo Marconi affected survival of the passengers and crew aboard the *Titanic*. An electrical engineer, Marconi constructed a system of long-range wireless communication, making it possible for ships at sea to communicate. By 1912, 589 ships were equipped with a Marconi Room that included a telegraph where wireless signals could be sent and received using Morse code, a system of dots and dashes that represent letters of the alphabet. At Captain Smith's request Jack Phillips sent out a distress call at 12:15 a.m. on April 15. The closest ship to hear the distress signal was the *Carpathia*, 58 miles away. The closest ship with wireless was the *Californian*, but its equipment was turned off for the night.

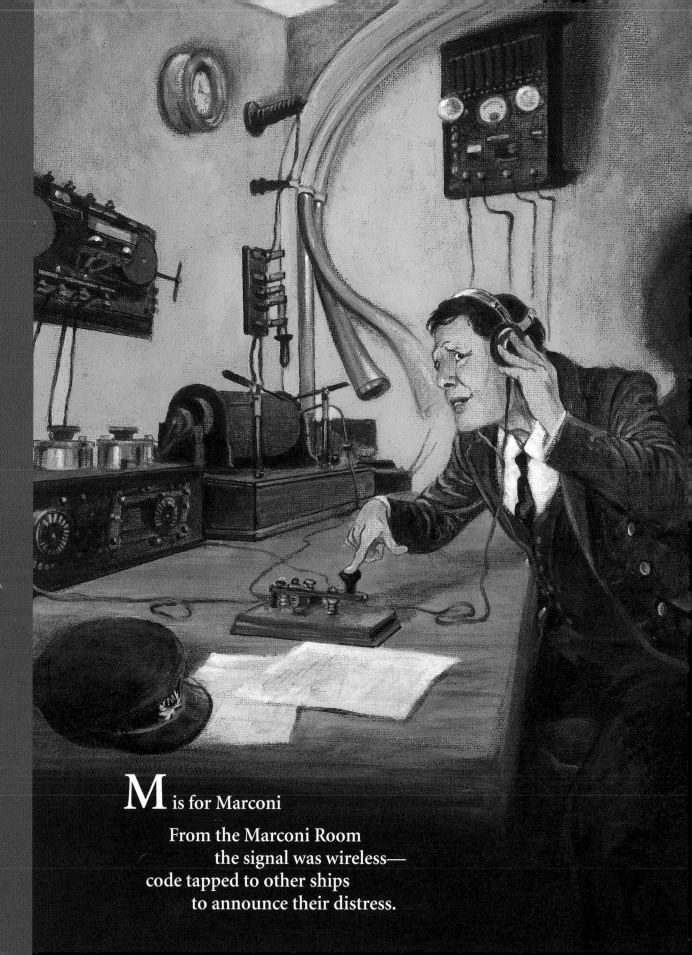

M m

M is for Marconi

From the Marconi Room
the signal was wireless—
code tapped to other ships
to announce their distress.

Second-class passengers were often professionals such as teachers and bankers. Their rooms had many of the comforts of first-class accommodations, but only wash basins and chamber pots. They did not have hot and cold running water or private baths.

An infamous second-class passenger was Michel Navratil, a tailor from Nice, France. He was one of 284 second-class passengers on the *Titanic*. Separated from his wife, Navratil boarded the ship under a false name, Louis M. Hoffman, and bought his two sons' tickets using false names Loto and Louis. His wife was unaware of their journey. On the fateful night, Navratil made sure both boys were placed into a lifeboat, but he remained behind and did not survive. Authorities in New York had trouble identifying the boys because of the false names. Their mother, still in France, eventually discovered their whereabouts through newspaper articles and was sent by the White Star Line to meet her sons and take them back to France.

N is for Navratil

Rescued in a lifeboat
were two French boys.
Saved with help from Father
it brought Mother tears of joy!

Lord Pirrie and J. Bruce Ismay needed more than one ship to meet their goal of providing large carriers for the Atlantic trade. Their plans called for the construction of three ships. The *Olympic* was built beside her sister ship the *Titanic* and was officially launched—without ceremony—as was the White Star Line custom, on October 20, 1910. The *Olympic* was a very popular ship far into the 1920s until eclipsed by the newer ships of that time period. After the *Titanic*'s sinking, the *Olympic* was extensively rebuilt for safety and returned to sea. She continued to make successful transatlantic crossings until the outbreak of World War I, at which time she was converted to a troop ship. After the war, she was refurbished and continued to serve as a passenger ship until 1935. The third ship was named the *Britannic*, which saw service in World War I as a hospital ship.

O is for *Olympic*

The *Olympic* was a sister ship
in the White Star Line.
Along with the *Britannic* she'd
make this company shine!

P is for Post Office and Postal Workers

A sailing post office
on a very large scale,
this ship carried nearly
seven million pieces of mail.

The *Titanic*'s official name was RMS *Titanic;* the RMS stands for Royal Mail Steamship. There was a sea post office aboard the ship. The onboard British and United States post offices employed a crew of five. The postal clerks spent their time checking, sorting, and distributing mail. On the fateful night of April 14th, the five men were celebrating a clerk's 44th birthday. The party came to an abrupt end when water gushed into the starboard side of the G-deck and into the sea post office. The clerks worked diligently to save approximately 200 mail sacks, dragging them to a higher deck to be rescued. The rising water was too fast, and more than 3,000 sacks of mail were lost—as well as the lives of the five clerks.

Q is for Queenstown

Titanic sailed from England,
then a port of call in France.
Her last stop was Queenstown
before Atlantic's vast expanse.

The *Titanic* set sail on its maiden (first) voyage from Southampton, England, on April 10, 1912. Its navigational route included two stops before entering the Atlantic Ocean for New York City. *Titanic* first stopped at Cherbourg, France, after a four-hour trip. Due to its postal obligations, there was an exchange of mail in addition to picking up and letting off passengers. At 11:30 a.m. the next day, the giant ship made its second stop in Queenstown, Ireland, known today as Cobh. Queenstown was traditionally the last stop for transatlantic ships. The *Titanic* remained anchored about half a mile or 3,000 feet from shore and passengers and mail were ferried to and from the ship in two tenders, or small steamships. Class of travel was also observed on the tenders, which meant that passengers remained separated even on the smaller boats.

Q q

R is for Rescue

As the *Titanic* went down
away from view,
the nearby *Carpathia*
helped in their rescue.

The rescue of *Titanic*'s passengers depended on other ships coming to their aid, but only the *Carpathia*, 58 miles away, made it in time to help. At 2:45 a.m., *Carpathia*'s captain, Arthur Henry Rostron, ordered rockets to be fired every 15 minutes. Survivors in lifeboats noticed the first one at 3:30 a.m. In response, the lifeboat passengers burned newspapers, letters, and other personal items to alert the rescue ship of their location. Rostron posted extra lookouts to carefully scan the dark seas, which held a large ice field and several icebergs. The *Carpathia*'s crew helped survivors onto the ship until 8:30 a.m. when the last lifeboat, no. 12, was brought alongside with nearly 75 passengers. An estimated 712 passengers and crew were rescued. An exact number is difficult to achieve due to record-keeping that included misspelled names and inaccurate information.

In the *Titanic*'s hour of need, the captain of the *Carpathia* gave orders that a dining room be used as a makeshift hospital; other rooms were opened to comfort survivors with warm blankets and food. The *Carpathia* set sail at 8:50 a.m. on April 15 for New York City to deliver the survivors to their final destination. The ship arrived at 9:00 p.m. on April 18, 1912.

S is for Captain Smith

In his darkest hour, when
Captain Smith feared the worst,
he ordered women and children
be put in lifeboats first.

The captain of the *Titanic* was Edward John Smith. Always interested in the sea, young Edward, known as E.J., began working in the harbor town of Liverpool, England, at the age of thirteen. In 1880, he joined the White Star Line, eventually achieving the high rank of commodore and commander of White Star's entire fleet of ships. Captain Smith's command of the *Titanic* was to have been his last for White Star Line before he retired after 32 years with the company. At 62 years old, Captain Smith was a popular man, especially with the wealthy, who would book voyages that had him at the helm. This led to Smith's nickname of Millionaire's Captain. On the fateful night, Smith was there to encourage passengers and crew alike to go into the lifeboats, though many refused. When the finality of the situation faced him, Smith chose to follow the unwritten rule for sea captains and went down with his ship.

Ss

T t

T is for *Titanic*

The RMS *Titanic,* in its day,
was a ship of luxury.
The events of April 1912
made naval history.

Lord Pirrie and J. Bruce Ismay's dream was a
fleet of giant vessels. To that end they chose
names that befitted that status. The word
"titanic" comes from Greek mythology and
refers to a legendary race of giants, called
the Titans. It was also White Star Line's custom to give its ships names that ended in
"ic" bestowing the sister ships the names,
Olympic and *Britannic.* This was done prob-
ably to rival the "ia" that Cunard used for
its ships, like the *Lusitania* and *Mauretania.*
The White Star Line was part of the
International Mercantile Marine, an American
conglomerate, a large group of companies,
all owned by financier J. Pierpont Morgan.
Morgan was the actual owner of the *Titanic*
and funded the building of the ship. The goal
of all concerned was to build a ship that
included the finest of the elegance and style
of the Edwardian era (1901–1910). They
spared no expense in craftsmanship and
materials when building the *Titanic.* Morgan
was devastated by the *Titanic*'s sinking,
and never recovered from it.

The day before the *Carpathia* docked in New York, U.S. Senator William Alden Smith proposed an official inquiry into the sinking of the *Titanic*. He wanted to discover what had gone wrong on the voyage, and what lessons could be learned to make ocean travel safer. During that time witnesses were asked questions about the life-saving devices aboard the ship, the ship's route and speed, and the crew's behavior. The Senate questioned 82 witnesses. The first was J. Bruce Ismay, director of White Star Line. They also questioned Second Officer Charles Herbert Lightoller, who spoke of Captain Smith's actions, and Harold Bride, one of two Marconi operators who had helped with distress calls.

The Senate made several recommendations for future passenger ship travel. For example, that there should be enough lifeboats to accommodate all passengers and crew. Regular lifeboat drills were to be conducted, as well as training for ships' crews in lowering and rowing lifeboats. Further, all ships should be equipped with two searchlights, and wireless stations would operate twenty-four hours a day. The International Ice Patrol was developed as a direct result of the *Titanic*'s sinking. This important group is now part of the United States Coast Guard. Its primary job is to find and report icebergs that might threaten ships' ability to sail through the North Atlantic shipping lanes.

U u

U is for U.S. Inquiry

For three weeks officials met—
a U.S. Inquiry—
finding ways for safer travel
aboard sailing ships at sea.

V

V is for Violinist

When *Titanic* was in danger
the violinist began to play
cheerful tunes like ragtime
to keep passengers' fears at bay.

Violinist Wallace Hartley was part of a small group of musicians who played on the *Titanic.* There were eight members playing in two groups: a string quintet (five musicians) and a trio (three musicians). They performed in the first- and second-class public areas.

Early on the morning of April 15, when Captain Smith realized the danger to all aboard, he ordered the groups to play light and cheerful music to help calm the passengers. They began playing at 12:15 a.m. in the first-class lounge on A-deck. The musicians then moved to the boat deck and played by the first-class entrance to the grand staircase. They eventually made their way outside, playing on the boat deck next to the gymnasium. The musicians played until after 2:00 a.m., when the tilt of the ship in its sinking made it impossible to continue. Many believe they heard the band playing "Nearer, My God, to Thee" as the ship sank, but others said they heard a popular waltz. All of the orchestra members perished with the ship.

Safety was a priority for shipbuilders Harland & Wolff. They built *Titanic*'s hull with a double bottom, and the hull was subdivided into sixteen compartments. The ship could remain afloat if two of the middle compartments or four of the front compartments flooded. Each compartment was equipped with a watertight door that sealed off the area. This feature led to the idea of the *Titanic* being "unsinkable." Unfortunately there was no easy way to make the areas above D-deck watertight due to a perceived need for large open areas to be used primarily for passengers. When the ship hit the iceberg, the impact caused the bow to flood, and sink under the weight of the water. Upon hearing that the ship had struck an iceberg, Captain Smith made sure that the watertight doors had been closed. Unfortunately, the rapidly flooding forward compartments were unable to contain the water, which spilled over the tops of the watertight compartments' bulkheads, compromising the watertight design, hastening the sinking of the ship.

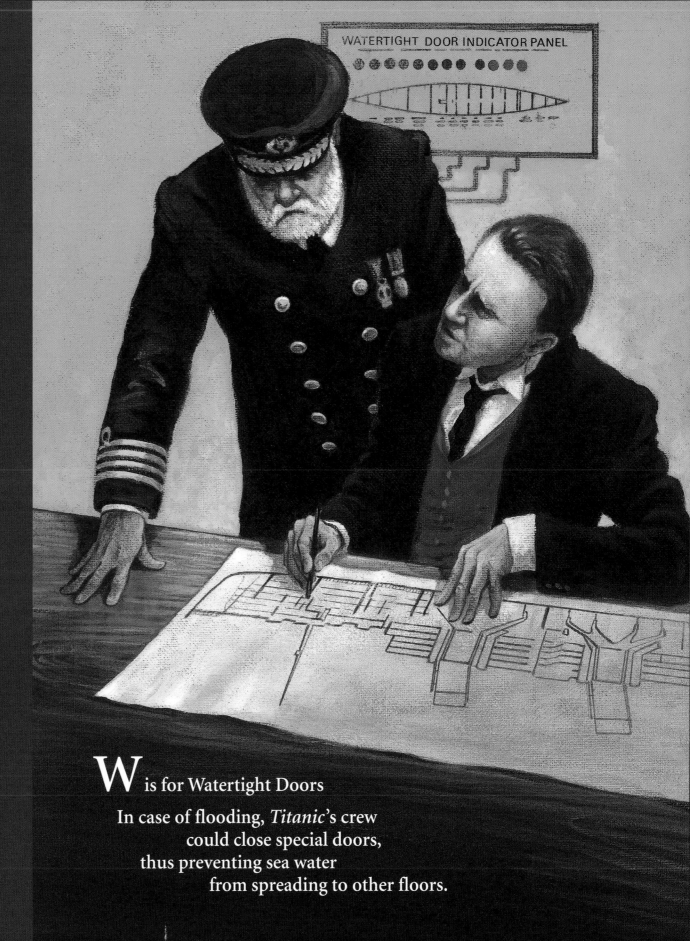

W is for Watertight Doors

In case of flooding, *Titanic*'s crew
could close special doors,
thus preventing sea water
from spreading to other floors.

X marks the spot where *Titanic* sank

An X is where *Titanic* was lost
and many sorrows remain.
Not until much later would
Titanic be seen again.

IRELAND

ENGLAND

• Queenstown

Southampton •

• Cherbourg

FRANCE

20°   10°   0°

X
X

After departing Southampton, England, on April 10, 1912, *Titanic* prepared to sail, with plans to arrive in New York City on April 17, 1912. It never reached New York but sank in the North Atlantic about 400 miles southeast of Newfoundland. *Titanic*'s distress call reported the location as latitude 41° 46' north, longitude 50° 14' west.

It has long been a goal of scientists who study the sea to explore and photograph the deepest parts of the ocean. Dr. Robert Ballard, an underwater geologist, and a team from the Deep Submergence Laboratory of the Woods Hole Oceanographic Institution in Massachusetts were able to do just that. The Massachusetts team, in a joint search with French scientists, found the *Titanic*'s wreckage on September 1, 1985. The following year, Ballard returned to the wreck site with the *Alvin*, a three-person submersible vehicle. On July 13, 1986, *Alvin* made a two-and-a-half hour descent of 12,500 feet, making Ballard and his crew the first people to see the ship in more than 74 years. They also deployed a small, remotely operated vehicle, the *Jason Jr.*, to explore inside the *Titanic*.

Yy

The year 2012 marks the one-hundred-year anniversary of the maiden (and only) voyage of the *Titanic*. Despite attempts to build better structures with the latest technology, disasters continue to occur. The people of 1912 felt the same way about the loss of lives that people today feel when jet planes, trains, or subway crashes occur. How do you pay respect to those who lose their lives in such horrific events? It's simply to tell their stories. With respect to the *Titanic*, that's what the Titanic Museum Attractions in Branson, Missouri, and Pigeon Forge, Tennessee, do every day!

Y is for the Years 1912 and 2012

The year 1912, the *Titanic* was lost.
Only a third would survive.
Telling their stories honors them
and keeps their memories alive.

Leo Zimmerman was one of approximately 706 third-class passengers aboard the *Titanic*. A farmer from Todtmoos, Germany, the 29-year-old left Europe for new opportunities in Saskatoon, Canada. His story was typical of many third-class passengers. They were immigrants looking for employment in the United States or Canada. Most of the third-class quarters were located on the F-deck and G-deck. Third class aboard the *Titanic*, while not filled with luxuries, was a comfortable way to make the transatlantic crossing. Passengers shared cabins, which came with two sets of bunk beds and a basin. They were served simple but hearty meals of soups, stews, meats, vegetables, potatoes, and bread. In their free time, third-class passengers played cards, danced on the deck or met friends in the third-class lounge, known as the general room. While about 200 third-class passengers were saved during the rescue, Leo Zimmerman was not one of the fortunate.

Zz

Z is for Zimmerman

Leo Z. traveled third class
befriending cooks and shoemakers,
playing cards with scholars,
while dining with miners and bakers.

In memory of those who did not survive

Debbie and Michael

—

ILLUSTRATOR ACKNOWLEDGMENT

Many thanks to Nikki Sisson, Martha Mikko Eicher, Geoff and Jane Gamble, Rachel,
Kelvin, Ben and Eli Potter, and Mrs. Derksen and Mrs. Knapp's second and third grade class.

Gijsbert

—

We invite all who read this book to join us in paying special recognition to Ed and Karen Kamuda—founders of
The Titanic Historical Society and noble caretakers of *Titanic*'s legacy for more than half a century.

Titanic Museum Attractions

—

Photo Reference for Painting of Mme. Navratil and sons (page N):
Library of Congress, Prints & Photographs Division,
LC-DIG-ggbain-12109 (digital file from original negative)

Text Copyright © 2011 Debbie and Michael Shoulders
Illustration Copyright © 2011 Gijsbert van Frankenhuyzen

All rights reserved. No part of this book may be reproduced in any manner
without the express written consent of the publisher, except in the case of brief
excerpts in critical reviews and articles. All inquiries should be addressed to:

Sleeping Bear Press
315 E. Eisenhower Parkway, Suite 200
Ann Arbor MI 48108
www.sleepingbearpress.com

Sleeping Bear Press is an imprint of Gale, a part of Cengage Learning.

10 9 8 7 6 5 4 3 2 1

Printed by China Translation & Printing Services Limited,
Guangdong Province, China. 1st printing. 07/2011

Library of Congress Cataloging-in-Publication Data

Shoulders, Debbie.
T is for Titanic : a Titanic alphabet / written by Debbie and Michael
Shoulders ; Illustrated by Gijsbert van Frankenhuyzen.
p. cm.
ISBN 978-1-58536-176-2
Special Edition ISBN 1-978-1-58536-792-4
1. Titanic (Steamship)—Juvenile literature. 2. Shipwrecks—North
Atlantic Ocean—Juvenile literature. 3. Alphabet—Juvenile literature.
I. Shoulders, Michael. II. Frankenhuyzen, Gijsbert van. III. Title.
GR530.T6S56 2011
910.9163'4—dc22   2010052909